My Body Needs
FOOD

by Jenna Lee Gleisner

amicus
high interest

Amicus High Interest is published by Amicus
P.O. Box 1329, Mankato, MN 56002
www.amicuspublishing.us

Library of Congress Cataloging-in-Publication Data
Gleisner, Jenna Lee, author.
  My body needs food / by Jenna Lee Gleisner.
    pages cm. -- (Healthy me!)
  Summary: "Introduces the benefits of healthy foods, the five food
groups, and how the digestive system works to turn food into energy for
our bodies while offering tips for a healthy diet."-- Provided by publisher.
  Audience: Age 6.
  Audience: K to grade 3.
  Includes index.
  ISBN 978-1-60753-587-4 (hardcover) -- ISBN 978-1-60753-687-1 (pdf
ebook)
  1. Food--Juvenile literature. 2. Nutrition--Juvenile literature. 3. Health--
Juvenile literature. I. Title.
  RA784.G55 2014
  613.2--dc23
                              2013046274

Photo Credits: Shutterstock Images, cover, 4, 7, 9, 10, 12 (top), 12 (middle),
12 (bottom), 22; Mathieu Boivin/Thinkstock, 2, 18; Sergey Novikov/
Shutterstock Images, 15; Ruth Black/Shutterstock Images, 17; Samuel
Borges Photography/Shutterstock Images, 21

Produced for Amicus by The Peterson Publishing Company
and Red Line Editorial.

Designer Becky Daum
Printed in the United States of America
Mankato, MN
1-2014
PA10001
10 9 8 7 6 5 4 3 2 1

TABLE OF CONTENTS

WE NEED FOOD

What did you eat today? We all need food. Healthy foods give us **energy**. They help our bodies grow.

Healthy Hint
Eat a healthy breakfast. It will give you energy to start the day.

VITAMINS

Healthy foods are full of **vitamins**. Our bodies need these to work well. We need them to grow, too. Milk has vitamin D. It helps bones grow strong.

FOOD GROUPS

Milk is in the **dairy** group. There are five main food groups. They are dairy, **protein**, fruits, vegetables, and **grains**.

Healthy Hint
This chart shows all five food groups. Eat foods from each one every day.

HOW MUCH?

Fruits are full of vitamins A and C. So are vegetables. Kids should eat one to two servings of fruits and vegetables each day.

Healthy Hint

Try dipping carrots in hummus. Hummus is made of vegetables. You will get two servings at once!

PROTEIN

Eggs are in the protein group.

Meats and nuts are, too. Our

bodies turn protein into energy.

This energy lets us run and play.

Our brains need protein to think.

DIGESTIVE SYSTEM

The **digestive system** breaks down food. The food turns into energy. The energy is sent to the whole body. Energy lets us be **active**.

JUNK FOOD

Junk foods are bad for the body. They do not have vitamins. And they are full of sugar and fat. Save junk foods for treats. Only eat a little bit.

17

18

HEALTHY SNACKS

Snacks are fun to eat. You can choose healthy snacks. Pick your favorite fruit. Mix it with yogurt to make a smoothie. A smoothie counts as a fruit and a dairy serving.

HEALTHY BODIES

Our bodies need healthy foods. They give us energy and help us grow. They also help our bodies work the best they can. What is your favorite healthy food?

GET STARTED TODAY

- Eat a healthy breakfast each morning.

- Eat foods from each of the five main food groups.

- Eat fruits and vegetables with other healthy foods, such as apples and peanut butter.

- Save sweets and other junk foods for special treats.

- Try making healthy snacks, such as smoothies.

WORDS TO KNOW

active – full of energy and busy

dairy – fluid milk and other foods that are made from milk, such as cheese and yogurt

digestive system – the body system that breaks down food so the body can use it

energy – the strength and ability to do activities without getting tired

grains – foods that are made from wheat, rice, oats, or other grains, such as bread, pasta, and oatmeal

protein – a chemical found in humans and living plants and animals; food protein includes foods that are made from meat, eggs, beans, peas, and nuts

vitamins – substances in foods that humans need for good health

LEARN MORE

Books

Head, Honor. *Healthy Eating*. Mankato, MN: Sea-to-Sea Publications, 2013.

McGregor, Emily. *Enjoy Your Meal: What Happens to Your Food When You Eat?* Vero Beach, FL: Rourke Publishing, 2008.

Web Sites

BAM! Body and Mind
http://www.cdc.gov/bam/nutrition/game.html
Play the Dining Decision Game to test your knowledge about healthy foods!

KidsHealth
http://kidshealth.org/kid/htbw/digestive_system.html
Learn more about how the body's digestive system works.

MyPlate Kids' Place
http://www.choosemyplate.gov/kids/
Play games and watch videos to learn more about healthy food choices.

INDEX